RILY

rily.co.uk

NO
PLACE
TO CALL
HOME

Published by Rily Publications Ltd, 2018
ISBN 978-1-84967-400-3
Copyright © Katey Pilling and Llinos Dafydd, 2018

The Quick Reads project in Wales is an initiative coordinated by the
Welsh Books Council and supported by the Welsh Government.
Printed and bound by CPI Group (UK) Ltd, Croydon, CR0 4YY

Cover design by Sion Ilar

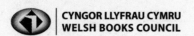

NO PLACE TO CALL HOME

Katey Pilling
and Llinos Dafydd

Introduction

This is Katey Pilling's story, a woman who has been homeless a few times in her life. It's been a roller-coaster ride, but the whole experience has shaped her as a person. Here, Katey gives her own take on homelessness, giving us a detailed account from her childhood in Aberaeron on the west Wales coast through to adulthood. We also hear about the frustrations that have left deep scars on her.

People think that you must have done something drastically wrong to become homeless – but in Katey's case, this is far from the truth. Now, she works for Shelter Cymru, a charity that has helped her over the years, a charity that wants everyone in Wales to have a decent home. They believe a home is a fundamental right and essential to the health and well-being of people and communities.

They work with people in housing need across Wales to prevent them from losing their homes by offering free, confidential and independent advice. When necessary they challenge the authorities on behalf of people, to ensure their clients get the right kind of help but also to improve practice and learning in the housing professions.

They work as equals with the people who use their services. Providing information, advice and support is key to helping people identify how to find and keep a home, and to help them take control of their lives. Shelter

Cymru also provide housing advice at community-based locations across Wales. People have always been at the heart of everything they do and they will continue to be driven by their founding belief that everyone in Wales has the right to a decent, secure home.

There are many complex reasons why people become homeless. The biggest cause is relationship breakdown with parents, family or partners where one person has to leave the family home. Other factors also play a part, such as unemployment, losing a job, poverty, rent arrears, drug issues, domestic violence or abuse, alcohol issues, poor health, mental health issues, mortgage arrears, eviction, and leaving care homes or other institutions without support.

There is some advice with useful phone numbers at the end of this book, but for now sit back and have a good read. Take a look at Katey's journey. Her honesty is a breath of fresh air.

*It's hard to be strong when we feel
we have no control of things that are
happening in our lives. Being homeless
can feel like that, quite out of our control.
Often we are at a chaotic crisis point
when we find ourselves potentially or
actually homeless, so staying strong is
half the battle. But we can get through
it. Even though we can't always see the
light at the end of the tunnel, it is there.*

1. A very different childhood

Imagine a childhood where you never know where you are going to lay your head down every night. Imagine a childhood where you have to walk from pub to pub in town after school, looking for your mother.

It happened to me. I was at school in Aberaeron at the time, and I well remember walking from door to door as streetlamps flickered to life, not sure where I'd find my mother this time, where I'd sleep that night. I never knew where she was, and I don't think she cared, either; she was always drunk, on whatever alcohol she could get her hands on.

Mum's alcoholism was the main reason we were homeless. We had moved to Aberaeron in 1987, when I was eight, leaving my three much older siblings up in Lancashire with my father. She and my father had split up when I was a year old. She'd struggled hard, doing her very best to make sure we were brought up well, but her alcoholism got the better of her.

I remember the day we hitchhiked down to Wales from Lancashire, me and her. We set off first thing in the morning, and it was a bright, sunny day. We had to wait two hours in Newtown, mid Wales, before someone picked us up. I must have been standing on a red ants' nest, because within five minutes of being in the car I

11

realised that I was covered in them and had been bitten several times.

'Ants! Ants!' I cried. 'Stop the car! Stop the car!'

All my mum and the gentleman in the front of the car could hear was me screaming and trying to smack my body. But eventually the car stopped and I shook the ants off my clothes at the side of the road.

Things took a turn for the worse when we got to Aberystwyth. It was getting late, getting dark. We'd been standing on the side of the road for a while when a car pulled up. A Robin Reliant, if I remember correctly. The driver told my mum that if she wanted him to give us a lift to Aberaeron, she'd have to leave me for a bit, and go around the corner with him. My mum told him to get lost. We only had £25. But because it was dark, and the man had scared us, my mum flagged down a taxi and we went to Aberaeron that way.

Aberaeron is a lovely seaside town, and the houses are painted all colours of the rainbow. It looks like a difficult place to be unhappy, but we managed it. Mum felt that we would settle well in the area, as we had friends in Aberaeron. As children we used to go on holidays there, and we spent a lot of our summers there. My dad lived in Lancashire, although he lived in Wales for a little while before he and my mum split up when I was a baby.

My mother opened an art gallery at first when we

arrived in Aberaeron. But it didn't do too well, and she chose to keep the gallery going rather than provide a roof over our heads. We lived in a caravan for a little while, but then we were homeless, moving from place to place. To cope with the stress, my mum turned to alcohol again.

Because she was drinking, everything was fine in her world. But to me it was a very unstable and traumatic time, because I never knew where we would be the next night. In the morning she would be ok, but at the end of the day I wouldn't be able to find her. It was horrible. School in Llwyncelyn was the only stable thing in my life at that point. But I never knew if she'd pick me up, or whether she'd be sober or not.

What little money we had was spent on drink, so I wasn't eating properly. I'd have to blag one of her drinking buddies for money to get a packet of chips. And then, of course, I'd have to think about where we were going to sleep that night and go around asking people if they had space on their floor. That period of my life gave me a lifelong fear of not having a home. The constant worry of how to keep a roof over our heads has stuck with me to this day.

After a few months of this I begged my mum to get in touch with the social services. I couldn't handle living the way we were any more. But rather than helping us find our feet in Aberaeron, near my school and my mother's art gallery, they moved us to a bed and breakfast in Llanarth,

13

five miles up the road. (Although at that point, the gallery was on its last legs anyway. Mum's life was too chaotic to keep it going.)

The B&B put a roof over our heads, but only for a few hours each day. The owner told us that we couldn't stay there between 10am and 5pm. It all became too much and we soon realised that there was nothing to keep us there, so we decided to leave Wales for a while.

We ended up moving up to Altringham, south-west of Manchester, where my nan lived, and spent nine months living in a hostel for homeless families. I had just turned twelve and it was a struggle at the hostel. We had a room but the kitchen and bathroom were shared, so we had to take turns. And we couldn't go anywhere at night, as the hostel locked its doors at 9pm.

The hostel was a big old grey building, I think from the Victorian era, and made to look very stern. It wasn't welcoming. Inside, the metal beds were grey, the walls were grey. It always felt dark and dingy, with no colour anywhere. It was worst in the shared kitchens where very little natural light got through.

I think there were sixteen family rooms over two floors, and families were grouped in fours to share one kitchen and one bathroom. The rules were strict, and if we spent more than a night or two away from the hostel we could lose our place there. I did befriend one young person who lived there, a boy named Conrad, who was there with his mum and dad. We used to walk to school together and home again.

Our room was quite large with two single beds and a set of bunk beds. I remember claiming the top bunk for my bed as it felt as if I wasn't really in the room, being that bit higher up, so I could pretend I had my own room and that life was normal.

It was very difficult for me in many ways, but especially as a very early starter when it came to physical changes. I'd started my periods when I was nine years old, so by the time I was in the hostel I'd already been dealing with that for a few years. It was very hard as children that young don't really know how to cope with it very well.

I remember being in the bathroom and asking my mother if I could use tampons as my periods were always very heavy, but she said I was too young. Sometimes things got really messy and I'd have embarrassing accidents, and as you can imagine, having to share facilities didn't make it easier.

At that time also, I started to suffer from breathing problems. My mum thought I was just acting up, and saying I was breathless to get out of going to school the next day. I was diagnosed with asthma in the end, but the fear of not being able to breathe and not knowing why certainly added to my anxiety.

I was also treated pretty badly at all the schools I went to. It's really hard to be the new girl, over and over again. Friendships were already established and most children didn't want me to be a part of their gangs. There wasn't any place for me. My mum was unconventional, and I didn't have the best of clothes. We never had any money, so I was always in hand-me-downs, and my uniform wasn't always right. I was always a target because I was different. As a defence mechanism, I tried to put on a false smile, and be loud and bubbly. But I was still a target.

Eventually one of my elder brothers managed to find us a terraced house in Burnley – a pretty grim place, two-up two-down, with the only toilet outside in the garden. While at the school there, I was bullied very badly, and got into a massive fight with the school bully. I wasn't a fighter at all and it scared me, so I stayed off school for five months. I refused point blank to go. The fear was awful. The walk home had been worse than being in school.

I missed an awful lot of education. Grammar was always difficult for me, as I was never taught it. Adverbs and nouns and stuff – it's only recently that I've learnt what they mean! And that was through my daughter, through her school work. There are so many gaps in my education. (I was diagnosed with dyslexia when I was sixteen, just before I sat my GCSEs, but I still managed to get five!)

I was a constant worrier, even though we now finally

had a house. But I was worried that my mum wouldn't be able to maintain the tenancy, because of what had happened in the past.

When I was around twelve I fell in with a group of born-again Christians, an evangelical group of people in Burnley. As silly as it sounds, being with them gave me the first feeling of being in a proper family that I'd had since I was very little. They showed me what a real family could be like, being part of a group that actually cared for each other. What they gave me was invaluable. I was fed, I was cared for and I was loved, in a way, and it meant the world to me. It showed me what life should be like.

However, the trauma of my childhood had taken its toll. At the age of seventeen I had very bad mental health problems, and tried to take my life three times. The first time, I took an overdose, and had to go to the hospital to get my stomach pumped. I was released the next day. Mum wasn't around at this point. She'd moved back to Wales with my stepdad, and left me in England. I overdosed again, and was admitted to hospital to get my stomach pumped once more. I was released again.

The third time I took an overdose they tried to section me but because I was under eighteen they had to get parental permission. I think I was there for three to four weeks before my mum came up, and she didn't give her permission, so I was released into her care.

Things eventually improved at home. My mother had found John, my stepdad, and she stayed with him for the rest of her life. He brought stability into our lives, which was fantastic. I was a little worried at first because he owned a pub in Burnley, and my mum's alcoholism had been such as issue for her. Mum had a job as a barmaid there. But her drinking had become much more manageable by then, especially during the time we were living at the hostel. She couldn't really drink like she did back in Aberaeron. And my stepdad wasn't a heavy drinker like she was.

John was our saviour in many ways. It was the first time in a long while that we had stability. He saved us from homelessness. Because my mum was up and down all the time, she never stuck to a job for long. But he always worked, he always had a job, so we always had a roof over our heads.

I try not to think about my childhood. There are some great memories, but there are some awful ones too. It's really difficult to look back on some of the hard times. But I think the adversities have shaped me as a person, too. Although I'm damaged in some ways, I'm stronger in others. Most importantly, I was determined that I never wanted my own child to go through the same chaos that I did, so when I became pregnant at twenty and had my daughter, I was determined that I would always be there for her, and that she would never go hungry. And I needed every ounce of this determination when we, ourselves, became homeless.

2. Stuck in a rut, again

Thankfully I had security for the first five years of my daughter's life. I'd moved to England to have Ellie, but when she was a year old I decided to move back to Wales.

We initially went to Llandysul, a small town in Ceredigion, and we were there for a while. But the accommodation wasn't suitable as it was damp, so we moved to the village of Drefach Felindre in Carmarthenshire for a year or so. But really, I wanted to be in Lampeter because I wanted to go to the university there.

I'd put my education on hold when I became pregnant. I'd been training to be a youth worker in Carmarthen at the time but gave it up before we moved to England. When Ellie was five months old, my partner and I split up and I became a single mother. So now, back in Wales, I felt that living near Lampeter would give me the chance to make more of myself and get the education that I really wanted.

We managed to get a house to rent in Betws Bledrws, which is a very small village about three miles from Lampeter. Happy days indeed. The house was nice but very isolated as there weren't any good transport links and I didn't drive at the time. We loved living there but it was hard as well.

When my daughter was a year and a half, I started to suffer from fibromyalgia (a condition that causes widespread pain), and my hands were so painful I couldn't actually use them. At that point I didn't get a diagnosis, only medication for the pain. At first it was just my hands that were affected, and they became so painful that I started losing muscle in them, further reducing my ability to do very much. It was a blow, and made me realise how important my hands are in almost everything I do.

The fibromyalgia started when I lived in Llandysul and by the time I was in Betws it had started affecting my legs, meaning I couldn't walk very far due to pain and fatigue. Doing basic things like washing up, cooking and eating were all hard and painful.

Unfortunately, my illness then got worse. It wasn't just in my hands and legs any more, I had pain in my back as well. We seemed far away from everywhere, with no buses around. But it was a nice little house, and a brilliant school for Ellie. The teachers were so supportive and loved having Ellie there as she was a sweet little girl who was always happy.

It was then that our situation nosedived. The lady that owned our house had moved to be with her family in England, but things didn't work out for her. So she wanted to come back. We had to give the house back. She gave me a Section 21 notice which is a notice to quit, and that gave us two months to leave the house.

By this point my health was getting very poor and we

were already struggling financially because I was unable to work, so I couldn't just save up enough money to find somewhere else to rent.

I didn't have a clue where to turn to as I couldn't seek help from my family. My mum had osteoarthritis and osteoporosis, and she was more or less crippled. John, my stepdad, became her main carer, and he had to give up work to look after her. Money was very tight for them. They couldn't afford to help me out, although they did help me out emotionally. My mum was there for me when she could be, although it was hard for us to see each other. I didn't drive then, and the public transport wasn't great. They lived in a caravan in Maesymeillion and there wasn't any room for me and Ellie.

My dad wasn't able to help me out financially either as he was always floating between jobs. It wasn't an option to ask any of my family for bond money or help with the rent, including my siblings who are twenty years older than me. It would have created a difficult situation if I'd asked for help, and borrowed hundreds of pounds. I simply wasn't in a situation to be able to pay them back. We were all from a working-class family background, and didn't have a lot of money behind us. For everyone, living from day to day was their main priority in life.

I ended up having to contact the council for help. Naively, I expected something to happen really quickly.

But back then, they couldn't help you before you were actually homeless. Now, you have 54 days before you're due to be made homeless to receive help and advice, but in those days it only started on the day you lost your home.

It was so stressful trying to work out how to save money, where to go next, and worrying about changing my daughter's school. Those two months of waiting to move out were very difficult. Luckily, Ellie was always an easy-going child, always had a smile and always wanted to help. And the head teacher at the school tried very hard to keep Ellie there, even looking for houses for us in the village and nearby so Ellie could stay. She went above and beyond to try and help so Ellie didn't have to leave the school.

On the day we had to move out, I had a phone call from Ceredigion County Council to say that they were going to set us up in a B&B in Newquay, west Wales. It was a shock, as it was far away from my daughter's school and my support network. I didn't drive, so it would be impossible to keep in contact with people. But hey – Newquay, sea, sand, ice cream – a dream come true for any child. Like a holiday!

But for me, reality kicked in. I had a three-bedroom house full of stuff. Where was I going to put everything? We had a dog as well, and nowhere for him to go. Sid, a Spaniel and Labrador mix, was a total nutter. He loved nothing more than chasing lights and was so naughty. We once found him in the neighbour's carp pond, just lying in the water, chilling out. He loved water and making a mess. Sid was just a big cuddly teddy bear and so patient with Ellie. She loved him. Thankfully a local sanctuary took him in for free, if we provided and paid for his food. The idea of losing the family dog as well as our home would have been devastating, especially for my daughter.

The B&B was great in one way as it was by the sea, and it was the summer holidays, so I could pretend to Ellie that we were having a fab holiday when, really, we weren't. She was only five years old at the time. One of the problems with the B&B was that we couldn't eat in our rooms and we only had a small communal area where we could eat. It was a B&B solely used by the council as temporary accommodation. The people who ran it weren't as nice as they could have been. Breakfast was very small, just a little carton of juice and a couple of slices of toast, even though they were being paid to provide a proper breakfast.

We shared with one family who had seven kids, so that made things difficult when it came to sorting food out. At one point, there were six families in the B&B, and we only had one microwave between us. I had thought that while we were in temporary accommodation, I would save some money by not paying any bills. I didn't realise how expensive it was to feed ourselves in a place where cooking wasn't really possible. Newquay is an expensive place to be, especially in summer. We had to have takeaways, or eat in cafés, or buy pre-packed sandwiches.

Then I was told by the authorities that we would be given shared accommodation in Lampeter. But a week went by, and we didn't hear another word from them. I phoned up but still nothing happened. We ended up staying in the B&B for around eight weeks, which I believe is over the limit for how long people are expected to be in temporary B&B accommodation.

My daughter should have been back at her old school by now but there was no way to get her there. I was so frustrated, I ended up having an argument with a housing officer – it was such a difficult time for us. They told me to prove that we weren't intentionally homeless, which was quite scary. I wouldn't have had any help at all if I'd been unable to prove that we weren't. That caused a lot of anxiety.

It was as if they were dangling a carrot in front of my nose and snatching it away at the last moment. We were living in limbo and it wasn't fair that they were raising our hopes. We didn't have a penny to our name and we were stuck in such a difficult situation.

However, we finally got into the shared house in Lampeter, which was a big Victorian terraced house, and we were the first people to move in, so that gave us time to find our feet. The first night we were there, the fire alarm started beeping and we couldn't turn it off.

It was unbearable! We phoned the council but they told us they couldn't help that night. As it used to be student accommodation, the fire alarm was very loud. Every few seconds we'd get another really loud beep and each time we hoped it would be the last one, but it didn't stop. It wasn't the best start!

When we were finally in, we took the ground floor, with a room for Ellie and a room for myself, on the same level as the kitchen, and a large garden. It was ok to start off with as my legs weren't too bad then.

Within a week or so another family moved in upstairs. These neighbours would have parties at the weekend, letting whoever they wanted into our shared spaces. The parties were loud, with people coming and going all the time and at all hours of the night, disturbing our sleep and making me anxious, as the only bathroom was upstairs above Ellie's room. It was a worry as we had no idea who these people were. Thankfully, the family moved out after a month or two.

Once they moved out I decided to move our things upstairs as that was where the only toilet was. I had Irritable Bowel Syndrome now, as well as mobility issues, so it made sense. Also, as there were three rooms up there I was able to make it into a kind of flat for us, with a bedroom each and a living room; the council were not happy about that as we were only allowed two rooms but I stuck to my guns.

IBS meant that I would sometimes need the toilet thirty or forty times a day, so I'd been getting exhausted when we'd been downstairs, going up and down the stairs so much that it was hurting my muscles. The pains in my legs were awful.

I wanted it to feel like home for my daughter and to try to give her some security. I bought a fridge and a microwave and a toaster that I put in our living area so that I didn't have to go up and down the stairs to the kitchen so much. My mobility was getting worse.

Another family soon moved in downstairs and we got on well with them. The mum had brought her dog with her, so we decided that we could get our dog from the kennels to live with us too.

The food situation was still difficult, there being just one kitchen, so we had to work around each other and try to cook when the other family wasn't using the kitchen. Again we ended up eating takeaways and ready meals as it was just too hard to always make food from scratch, so any money I hoped to save for a house was eaten up! It wasn't just food we had to buy though, because with all our stuff in storage we had to get many basics again (I couldn't drive and was too ill in any case to get to our storage and retrieve our own things).

Christmas was quickly approaching and I had no idea what I would do. We couldn't have our normal Christmas as we had no decorations, no tree and very little money, as well as limited access to the kitchen. So while I wanted to make it as normal as possible for Ellie, I didn't see how I could do that.

I don't remember what I bought her but it wasn't much as we had no space for things. The living arrangements were very cramped. Ellie ended up going to her father's on Christmas afternoon so she would have a normal Christmas with family around her. That was very hard for me as I wanted to be with her, but I knew it was best for Ellie.

On a happier note, that first Christmas morning in temporary accommodation I got up extra early and went into Ellie's room to say Happy Christmas. All I saw was a little girl under a mountain of wrapping paper, fast asleep. I'd expected her to be awake already but she must have woken in the night, saw that Santa had left some presents in her stocking and opened them; and then the excitement must have been too much so she had zonked out again with her little bum in the air!

Even so, it was a really subdued Christmas with not many presents to go around. It broke my heart to see my daughter having to live like this but I think she hardly noticed the difference. I had done my best to make it fun for her, but for me it was a really depressing time; all I could think about was how I'd let my daughter down.

By this time, we had been in temporary accommodation for around six months. I never expected to be homeless this long and had no idea how much longer we were going to be there.

I think the hardest part for me was not being able to feel secure; we never knew who else would be in the house and as I'd decided to move us upstairs, we were next to the bathroom. I had nightmares about strangers going into my daughter's room during the night, and that I wouldn't be able to protect her. I couldn't leave my daughter's bedroom door open like I would have at home but I couldn't lock her door either.

Ellie developed sleeping problems; she was unable to sleep when she should have and woke extremely early, no matter what time she went to bed. I know this was down to her feeling insecure as well as the noise of other people living in the house with us. I even got the health visitor out to see if we could help her. To this day – and she is seventeen now – she still has trouble sleeping. Some nights, she has barely any sleep.

We ended up staying in the shared house for around a year and a half. Due to my illnesses, we were very difficult to house. My doctor said we needed a bungalow or ground-floor accommodation, so the wait was long. Three families came and went whilst we were there and I must admit to feeling very jealous and quite bitter. It felt like we had been forgotten.

Eventually we were moved into a first-floor flat. I think the council just wanted to get us out of there and it wasn't a good move. Social services had to become involved as I was now classed as disabled and couldn't manage the stairs; I was even more isolated than before. My legs were really bad, and of course, we had to go up a set of stairs to reach the flat. It was a difficult place to live. I was physically struggling, and had to sit on the stairs and shuffle down to answer the door, and reverse the whole process to go back up again. Looking after myself was becoming harder and harder.

We were there for a few months, until a bungalow became available in Llanwnnen, only three miles from Lampeter. Hallelujah – at last! Originally designed for an elderly couple, it was such a relief for us to move in there and know that it would be our home for as long as we wanted it. We wouldn't have to leave because somebody wanted their house back. It was the security we needed. It was our paradise, our little palace, it was ours. And no one else was there – nobody walking in and out, nobody to have to share the amenities with.

We're still there now, ten years on. I'm still scared though, and the anxiety of perhaps having to go and live somewhere else is huge. I don't know if I could ever move from here.

3. I have no shame talking about it...

Being homeless is a soul-destroying experience. It makes you feel as though you've failed, that what you do is just not good enough. It's something I never want to go through again. The pressure to provide is great and when you can't do that you feel as though you are nothing.

It was a mixture of emotions for me to be homeless with my daughter, because although I'd been there before, this time I had Ellie to think of as well. It scared me because I'd promised myself that I wouldn't put my daughter in the same situation that I'd been in. I felt that I wasn't a good parent, even though it wasn't my fault. So I felt guilty, and that I hadn't tried my best. Yes, it was miles different from when my mum and I were homeless, because I wasn't drinking and doing all these things my mother had been doing, but it still made me feel that I wasn't good enough and that I'd failed as a mother.

There's a stigma attached to being a single parent anyway. To find myself homeless as well seemed a double whammy of guilt and shame. People think that I must have done something wrong to be in this situation: why couldn't I put a roof over my child's head?

That's a lot to deal with. I kept up a brave face for my daughter but I was really depressed. It was a situation which was out of my control and there was nothing I could do to change it. But to my daughter, I portrayed it in a much more positive way, as an adventure, almost, and she coped really well. I didn't make it an issue. It was my job to worry about it, not hers. However, my state of mind at the time was chaotic. I suffer from anxiety and depression anyway, but the whole situation left me really down in the dumps. When there's a child involved, it's a constant worry.

One thing which has stuck with me since I myself was a child is how cruel children can be. When I was first homeless, in my first year at comprehensive school, I had two friends, and I confided in them that my mother and I were homeless, but they just laughed at me. One said, 'I've put a penny in the Save the Children box, so you're going to be fine!' I just sat there, and all of a sudden it washed over me that my best mates were laughing at me because I didn't have a place to call home. It had taken me a lot of courage to talk to them. It's so hard for children, it really is. Obviously, the situation had been completely out of my hands, and none of it was my fault. For such good friends to ridicule me made me feel stupid, so from then on I didn't want to talk about my situation.

Now I'm thirty-eight years old and have been through homelessness again with my daughter, I'm not ashamed to talk about it. But at the time, I didn't talk. You judge yourself, whether it's your fault or not, whatever the circumstances. And you think other people are judging you in the same way.

When you're letting your child down in one of the biggest ways possible – which is not having a home for them – then your self-judgement can be an awful lot worse than anything anyone else can say to you. So I didn't really tell people that we were homeless. Maybe I told some that we were in temporary accommodation, but I didn't go out of my way to explain.

There are so many ill-informed assumptions, based on ignorance. If you have children, you can't be homeless; if you've been in the armed forces, you can't be homeless; if you've got a job and you're doing everything right, you can't become homeless. But in fact, statistically, there are a lot of families out there homeless, not necessarily on the streets but in temporary accommodation, some in places that are completely unsuitable for them because there's nothing else out there for them. These days, money isn't going as far as it used to. Wages have stayed the same, but the cost of housing and everything related to that, like heating your house and feeding your family, has risen, and sometimes the situation becomes impossible.

There are many degrees of homelessness. Being on the streets is obviously the worst situation you could find yourself in, but you can be homeless in temporary accommodation too. If you look up the definition of homelessness, it says 'the state of having no home', rather than 'you've got no roof over your head'. When we were homeless, yes, we always had a roof over our heads, but nothing was 'ours'. We couldn't relax in a place where other people were coming in and out and everything was shared. It became a situation where we were on tenterhooks all the time. Arguments would break out because there was washing-up in the sink, as we'd just taken our food upstairs to eat, and hadn't washed up before doing so. In most households, you eat your dinner first, and then do the washing up. But in a shared household, small things like that can make people angry. It's understandable, as they've got to use the kitchen too. A normal day-to-day life is completely impossible. My illness didn't make things easy either. When I wasn't feeling strong enough to do something – tough. I had to do it, or we would have been kicked out.

The whole concept of homelessness and the stigma that goes with it includes the assumption that it's always your fault; that you've done something wrong to be in that position. And people don't usually know what to say. Socially we became isolated. We had no phoneline, no credit to put on the mobile phone. When we were sent to the B&B in Newquay, it was really hard. Most of my friends didn't drive so there was no way for them to come and see us, and vice versa. We were stuck, while everybody else was getting on with things. I didn't have anybody to turn to, despite my support network in Lampeter.

On my Facebook feed a few months ago somebody was talking about 'these bad choices' people make to end up being homeless. I didn't make any bad choices in the run-up to being homeless with my child. Not all homeless people have done something to deserve to end up on the streets. But unfortunately, that blaming attitude is still widespread.

It really gets me down, and I most certainly have already had a lot of downs due to homelessness. I think one of my lowest points was when the second family was moved out of the shared Lampeter house into their own new home, perhaps just over a year after we'd been there. It felt like we had been forgotten, that we were never going to be rehoused and that we weren't in enough need. I couldn't help comparing our situation with theirs.

Wasn't my little family just as needy as them? Did we do something wrong? Why did we have to keep on living there when others came and went? Were we being punished for something that I didn't know about, or did the housing department just not like us?

It was a really hard time and I questioned everything, and I think that due to this my anxiety and depression went through the roof. I found myself feeling hopeless and that our situation would never end, and I felt powerless to change what was going on. I really didn't have the money to move us into private rented accommodation, even though I thought that I'd be able to save up whilst living there. But saving up was never going to happen. The small amount I had coming in went as soon as I had it because of the hidden expenses of living in temporary accommodation.

And even when I had managed to put a little aside, something always happened which meant I'd have to spend it. I would try to stay at friends' houses at the weekend as I just couldn't face going back to the house, but I felt really uncomfortable, like I was imposing on people, and I was really scared that I would outstay my welcome. I think because of that I ended up isolating myself. I didn't want to see my friends or family, something I usually feel when I sink into a depression. I feel like I'm in the way and it's best for me to stay away from everyone, and that people will just get fed up with me being in such a dark place and won't understand.

With hindsight, it is typical depression mentality, but you don't always see it at the time, and then you become accustomed to being insular and it's so difficult to pull out of it. I know now that when I start avoiding social situations I need to look at my mental health, but I think I was so far down the hole then that I couldn't see daylight.

I've always thought of myself as an optimistic person.

I had a difficult childhood, and to get through it I used to daydream about what could happen, what might happen, what I'd like to happen. Being able to do that really helped me through difficult situations. I'm always hoping things will get better or an answer will come along to fix problems.

In Lampeter, I had no choice in the end but to get through things, and survive. If I wasn't strong for Ellie, what sort of a mother was I? Because of my daughter, I constantly had to battle through; there was no other option. I had to make the best of the worst of situations. I was never going to give up. Even being homeless, if Ellie was suffering, I wasn't doing my job. I had to get through things for both our sakes.

I've had mental health problems since I was a teenager, and over the years I've learnt how to cope. I've learnt to recognize the symptoms. If I feel depressed, or if I feel that I'm about to go down a slippery slope mentally, I always go to see my GP and talk things through.

While in the shared accommodation in Lampeter I had great assistance from Cerecare, who support people with disabilities. I had a support worker, and they helped me out an awful lot, especially in dealing with paperwork, as well as helping me emotionally. It was nice to know that I had someone on my side.

Of course, Shelter Cymru means the world to me these

days. But before I sought help from them, it was a struggle. It was a waiting game, every day hoping I would get that phone call to tell me that we would be housed. As each day went by, and still no word came from the council, I felt so alone, as if nobody cared at all. I was told I was high priority, but it was still such a long wait.

I had friends I could talk too, and offload my worries onto, but I really didn't like to do that too much because I didn't want to moan all the time. Everyone has their own worries, and I didn't want to be a burden on anybody. My friends are great, but at the end of the day, I didn't want to push them away by complaining all the time.

So it was a rollercoaster of emotions, and to some extent still is. Even now, I'm very anxious, though I have a roof over my head, and a home. I know from experience that circumstances can take it all away in an instant. I don't think that fear will ever go away.

4. Homelessness happens to normal people...

Once we were settled in our new home I was able to get a degree in Anthropology and I graduated in 2014. At long last I had time to concentrate and better myself, and I felt that it was a natural step to do a course at Lampeter University, right on my door step. I was determined to achieve that degree, and prove that I was worth something. It was tough, due to my disabilities, and also working around Ellie, but I got through it. But I realised soon after I graduated that I was a little lost. I didn't know what to do with myself.

There I was in a little two-bedroom bungalow with a large garden. For us, it was perfect. Yes, the house could get a little cramped, especially as my daughter got older, but it was our space. We didn't have to share with other families. Home, sweet home.

The village we are in is nice and quiet but it took me a while for it to sink in that this was really my home. I didn't fully unpack everything for several years. I always had that dreadful feeling that we might have to leave again, that it wasn't permanent. I have to admit that there are still a couple of boxes unpacked. Perhaps it's a bit neurotic, but nothing felt stable for years. However, ten years later, we are still here.

So I was feeling restless, and decided to look into volunteering; I wasn't in a position to seek full-time work because of my health issues. I had to start somewhere, and I needed something in my life apart from being a mother, or a disabled person. I wanted to live a life, and not be stuck within the same four walls, day in day out. That would have led to depression which has always been a part of my life. I just knew that I mustn't get stuck in a rut, once again getting lost in my own thoughts. Depression can take away your motivation and your confidence. When I was suffering it took away my happiness, leaving me in a hole where not much light got in. It's a dangerous combination having self-esteem issues and health problems – so I had to be kind to myself, and really motivate myself to think positively.

Shelter Cymru had helped me when I was homeless, so naturally I wanted to volunteer with them – and once the ball got rolling, I never looked back. I'm now actually employed by them as a research officer.

I was a volunteer to start off with, with the Take Notice project, where we worked hand in hand with local authorities to improve their housing and homelessness services. We did tasks like evaluating websites and letters, and would even mystery shop the service to say what we felt were good practices, as well as identifying areas that could be improved.

Each Take Notice member had either been homeless or threatened with homelessness and had used local authorities to help them. Around six months after joining the project I was asked if I'd like to be a peer researcher for Shelter Cymru's policy and research team.

A lot of the research work involves data compiling, which includes conducting interviews with people who have been affected by homelessness.

In 2015 I worked on a survival guide for temporary accommodation with Shelter Cymru (see Chapter 5). I was able to use my experience to try to help other people in the same situation as we had been. The guide gives practical tips on how to make the situation as bearable as possible, such as keeping all your documents in one place, being prepared to cohabit, taking photos of your temporary accommodation when you move in so that if there are any arguments about damage you have evidence, and understanding that you may have to move on very quickly.

With the Take Notice project, we also performed a myth-busting role, where we challenged people's concept of homelessness. We did things like community talks, school talks and short information films telling our story of homelessness to combat the stigma associated with the issue.

It's not just a matter of giving something back to

Shelter Cymru for their help; I've found it's made a huge difference to me as well – to my self-confidence and my sense of self-worth. Before I started to work for Shelter Cymru, I didn't really think I was fit for anything. I didn't think I was able to do anything meaningful. Working for them has given me the ability to talk to people, even in conferences in front of hundreds of people. If you had asked me four years ago to do something like that, I would never have had the confidence. It's given me the boost I needed. I know that what I have to offer is worthwhile, and worthy.

And you know what? Homelessness happens to normal, everyday people. It doesn't have to be an old alcoholic on a street or an addict, or someone who has done something bad. It could happen to you, your next-door neighbour, your friend or a very dear member of your family. It happened to me, and it was completely unfortunate. One day I was happy, with a roof over my head, then the next – WHAM! It was all gone.

Sending that email to Shelter Cymru asking for volunteering opportunities was one of the best thing I've ever done. The training aspect was huge for me. I learnt so many things. When I was asked to become a peer researcher, I was over the moon – it was my first paid job for a very long time. Because of the limitations I have due to my illnesses, I didn't think an employer would value me or what I could give because there would be so many times when I'd have to say that I couldn't do things. So the fear of rejection had always been there. But being asked to do this job rather than applying for it was so flattering. It was out of the blue as well. It gave me new confidence. That was the beginning for me.

Two years ago I went to the Houses of Parliament and gave a speech on homelessness in front of fifteen Welsh MPs. That was the first time I'd stood up and given a speech in such a setting, talking about my experiences. I was blown away. This was me, Katey, who had been through homelessness, who's disabled, and who has always seen herself as somebody who 'can't' do things. And yet there I was! Opportunities like these from Shelter Cymru have really built me up and shaped me, and completely changed how I see myself. It's given me confidence, and I now know that my brain is still useful, even if my body isn't! I can still make a difference using my voice to help other people – and sometimes using my voice to talk on behalf of others who don't think they have a say in this world.

When you're in a situation where homelessness is an issue, it's a really chaotic time, and you may not be firing on all cylinders. Having someone on your side, someone who can speak up for you, can make all the difference between spiralling into a pit of depression and anxiety and self-loathing, and staying strong.

One of the first paid jobs I did for Shelter Cymru was to present the work we'd done in front of a roomful of people at a conference. I was given just half an hour's warning. Oh my goodness – the stress! But I had to say yes, although I've never been a public speaker. I was shaking but knowing what I was talking about – my own experience – made it easier. In fact it felt good. I wasn't just that Katey who sat at home looking at the same four walls any more. I did it, and I got through it. And I was named the best speaker of the day on the feedback forms! It was such a boost. Since then I've done many speeches in front of hundreds of people, and also small ones in hostels. I don't feel scared any more, whereas at the beginning I always doubted myself.

Shelter Cymru has given me my self-belief back. I'm more than just my broken past. That's a huge thing for me. It means that I'm able to be a voice for others who are in the same situation I was in. The work that we do with local authorities is rewarding as well. Conwy have taken our recommendations on board. They have evaluated their website and the letters they send out and they've implemented changes to them. People at risk now, who are potentially homeless, are benefiting from what I and other project members have been through. We are making the service easier and better.

I've visited different local authorities and spoken to

housing officers about my experience of being homeless, explaining what the weaknesses are in the system and what could be done to improve things. To be given that opportunity, and know that our suggestions will directly affect how other people are helped, is a huge thing.

I may have had bad situations in my life, but through Shelter Cymru I've been given an opportunity to turn things around, and create something positive. I've learnt the know-how. How to present, how to speak, and how to be an advocate for other people. Shelter Cymru have opened up my world.

It may be a cliché, but when I first started I was like this little blind caterpillar. I didn't know what I was doing. But during the last three years, I actually became a chrysalis and now I've turned into a butterfly, and I can fly wherever I want, as they've given me the wings to reach wherever I need to go.

But where next? My daughter is going to university in a few months, and hopefully it will be my time to shine. Since becoming a parent, any physical energy I have goes into looking after my daughter, and making sure she has everything she needs. But once she's in university, even though I'll still be a mum to her, she won't be around for me to worry about feeding and looking after her on a day-to-day basis. I won't have to put all my energy into being Mum. I had Ellie when I was twenty-one and to some extent since then my own life has been put on hold. And of course, my illnesses on top of everything else have limited me. But hopefully I can branch out now and see what's out there for me, because I won't be needed so much.

One thing is for sure, I will stay in my home, sweet home. The home that I have now means the world to me, ever since the days we were given the keys. On that day, I had my real dad by my side – and that was the last time I saw him. We knew he had cancer but didn't know he was dying. On the day I had the keys, he came down to Wales to visit us, and he drove us to see the house for the first time. He was so chuffed. We went out for a meal that night, and that was the last time I saw my dad alive.

I think he knew deep down it would be the last time he would ever get to Wales. It was my dad's final farewell. He visited all the places he loved when he used to live here with my mum before they split up; places where he'd once lived, the people who had been part of his life. Our family had always loved this part of Wales and when things got too much in Lancashire, this was where we always came. It was the same both for my parents and myself – we were always torn between Lancashire and west Wales.

I remember on that last trip to Wales, my dad and I visited my mum and stepdad in their caravan. It was a lovely sunny day and as my dad sat outside looking to the Cambrian Mountains in the distance, he said, 'I can die a happy man now; there is nothing as beautiful as this.'

My house means a lot more to us than just being our home. It was fitting that Dad was the one who took me to see the house, and he still feels a part of things, because it was the beginning of our new journey – a beautiful journey that hopefully will never end.

5. Getting by

Here's some advice from Shelter Cymru, and a survival guide for when you're homeless:

1. If and when you're offered temporary/new accommodation:

→ **Make a note of your new address.** Put the full postal address in your phone or diary as you are probably going to be asked for it many times.

→ **Take pictures.** If there is any visible damage or disrepair, then get evidence. You do not want to be billed for them at a later date.

→ **Before you move in:** label all your boxes/bags and pack them so you can easily find the items you use the most.

→ **On arrival:** make a note or take a photo of electricity, gas and water meter readings. There are many different types of meter, so make sure you are familiar with the type you have and ask the landlord or agent how to use them. Get them to run through how the heating and hot water works. Make sure the water supply is on and find out where the stop-cock is – you never know when you will need it!

→ **Find out about the local area.** Find the GP, supermarkets, convenience stores, leisure centres, parks and play areas. Food can be expensive – find out where the food banks are if you need them.

→ **Join the local library.** You can use their computers to access the internet and your emails.

→ **Make sure you know the rules.** Make sure you are given a copy of the house rules, if there are any. People can get caught out; don't be one of them. Whatever you think of them, they are the rules, so don't fall foul of them.

→ **Be prepared to cohabit.** You may find yourself sharing kitchens, bathrooms and communal areas. This can be a source of tension but stay calm and talk to support workers, staff or others if any situations arise.

→ **Be sensible with your money.** Living in temporary accommodation can be more expensive than living somewhere more permanent. If things get financially tough there are sources of help available, such as the Discretionary Assistance Fund or Discretionary Housing Payments. Find out if you are entitled to any benefits or grants that can help you. Most importantly, if you are falling into debt, seek help.

→ **Be prepared to move really quickly.** The process of finding permanent accommodation can be slow but when things happen they move fast. Keep a few boxes spare – you always end up with more bits and bobs than you think. Look out for 'white van man' phone numbers and when a house or flat becomes available, you'll be ahead of the game.

2. Standing up for yourself

→ **Make sure the accommodation you're offered is suitable for your needs.** If the accommodation is not suitable, seek independent advice before you turn it down – otherwise there is a risk the local authority might not fulfil their duty towards you.

→ **Use your voice.** Don't just sit and wait for things to happen. Contact your housing officer regularly, find out what's happening with your case and discuss any problems. However, be respectful. Making a point politely will be better for you in the long run.

→ **Keep on top of your Housing Benefit.** Make sure you let the Housing Benefit department know of any changes of circumstance. Follow up to be certain that changes have been made.

→ **Get evidence.** Things get lost so keep as much evidence as you can. Get receipts or photocopies of all the forms you hand in. You can use the library to scan documents and save them to your email. Scanning is free, photocopies cost per sheet. Also, keep a note of dates, times and people's names so that you can give exact information about your case.

→ **Keep it safe.** Make sure that all your paperwork is in the same place. A few seconds of simple filing can save you a major headache later on.

→ **Pick and choose your battles** but be prepared to compromise with the local authority, support workers and other tenants.

3. Getting support

You are not alone. If you feel you or your family are suffering, speak to someone. There are organisations out there that can help if you feel you are being treated unfairly. (See below.) It's better to get things dealt with ASAP.

And finally...

→ **Don't be discouraged.**
→ **Don't be ashamed of what's happening – homelessness can happen to anyone.**
→ **Don't cut yourself off from friends and family.**
→ **Don't be afraid to speak up if you have a question or complaint.**

Useful numbers

Shelter Cymru is Wales's people and homes charity. They provide independent specialist advice, advocacy and legal representation for anyone with housing problems. They also have specialist debt and money advisers available by phone, online or face to face. **Helpline: 0345 075 5005**

Citizens Advice Bureau provides free, confidential and impartial advice. They can help with a number of issues including money, benefits, housing or employment problems. **Helpline: 03444 77 20 20**

CALL: Community Advice & Listening Line is a mental health helpline for Wales, providing emotional support, referral to agencies and free self-help leaflets. **Helpline: 0800 132 737**

Samaritans is a free, confidential telephone service which is available 24/7 to anyone who needs to talk about what is happening or how they're feeling, and helps them find their own way forward. **Helpline: 08457 90 90 90 (24:7) Cymraeg: 0300 123 3011 (from 7pm to 11pm only, 7 days a week).**

6. Educate yourself

What does it mean to be homeless in Wales today? Here, Shelter Cymru explains...

Shelter Cymru is Wales's people and homes charity. We are here to prevent homelessness and bad housing. Each week we hold over 70 surgeries across Wales where people come to us for advice and support when faced with housing and homelessness issues. We also have a team of legal advisers who provide an advocacy service in county courts where we represent clients free of charge during eviction and repossession proceedings. We have a Shelter Cymru Live helpline and an online advice service. Last year we helped nearly 19,000 people and a further 142,000 online.

We're a homelessness prevention charity so we help people fight for their rights, get back on their feet and find and keep a home. Keeping people in their home is a priority for us. We have various advice and support services, as listed above.

Shelter Cymru is here to assist and support people who are faced with homelessness and all our services are free of charge. We work closely with Housing Solutions teams in all local authorities to help prevent homelessness.

We would advise people who are faced with homelessness to seek advice as early as possible. Shelter

Cymru is here to support people so that nobody has to face homelessness alone.

We also advise people who are already homeless to seek help – it's never too early or too late to seek assistance and there is help available. Individuals need the right support from specialist services, and Shelter Cymru can help in directing them to the appropriate agencies. Our underlying message is to keep trying, and not give up.

Rough sleeping is on the rise in Wales as is the pattern across the UK. Last year, Shelter Cymru saw an increase of 68% in rough sleepers and saw that homelessness on the whole is also increasing. While the number of households threatened with homelessness has gone up by 29% in the last year, the number that are actually homeless has increased by an astonishing 58%, to 10,884 households.

Mention the word 'homeless' and many people think of rough sleeping. The reality is that rough sleeping is only a part of the picture. Every year in Wales more than 25,000 people become homeless, including over 4,700 children. Of all those people, a few hundred will be living on the streets. The rest will be 'hidden' homeless – staying with family or friends; sleeping on friends' sofas; living in temporary accommodation provided by the council (bed and breakfast establishments and hostels); or else living in homes that are in very poor condition, or unsuitable for their needs.

A further 13,000 people a year come within days of losing their home and are only able to avoid homelessness thanks to the hard work of council homelessness services and other agencies such as us, Shelter Cymru.

Not enough people understand that the reasons for homelessness are to do with the economy and the system. There is also a lack of mental health services and drug addiction services to help certain people. We fully appreciate that finding and keeping a home is expensive and complicated, and we try to educate people that the reasons behind homelessness are complex and not the individual's fault.

With an ever-increasing demand for our services, we are looking at ways to increase the number of people that we help each year. Why do people become homeless? It's complicated, and it differs from person to person. But there are two main types of reason why people become homeless. Problems in the person's own life – such as physical or mental health conditions, relationship breakdown, or drug and alcohol misuse. And also problems in the system – such as the rising cost of housing, the poverty trap, and welfare benefit cuts brought about by the government.

Over the last 35 years Shelter Cymru has seen the housing crisis play a bigger role in creating homelessness. There aren't enough affordable homes being built, and this makes housing more expensive for everyone – including you.

With rent levels rocketing and home ownership an increasingly impossible dream, it's no wonder that so many families are struggling. But homelessness would never happen to you or me, would it? You'd be surprised. People from all walks of life are at risk.

True, having a low income is a major risk factor – but being in paid work is no guarantee. Last year nearly 19,000 people used Shelter Cymru's services and more than one in four of them had a job.

This is why you need to think carefully about the language you use. For example, Shelter Cymru would never use the term 'the homeless' because this makes people seem less than human. Homeless people are people first and foremost.

Here are some common facts about homelessness. They've been produced by people who've been there, especially for Shelter Cymru, and who know what they're talking about.

FACT! People become homeless for many different reasons. These could include: being evicted by your landlord; losing your job; health problems; relationship problems.

Even if you think that you are financially secure and would never be in a position where you might lose your home, sometimes homelessness can be caused by events completely outside of anyone's control such as fire or flooding.

FACT! Homelessness can, and does, happen to people from every walk of life. In Wales the biggest causes of homelessness are relationship breakdown, parents not being willing to accommodate, and the loss of a private tenancy – ordinary life events that could affect anybody. Homelessness could happen to anyone...

→ In Britain someone loses their home every 11 minutes.

→ 3.8 million families in the UK are one pay cheque away from losing their home.

FACT! It's true that households with children have more rights to get rehoused with help from the council than single people. But the shortage of affordable housing affects everybody and can lead to families spending long periods in emergency accommodation.

→ In Wales, more than 1,800 households were living in temporary accommodation at the end of 2015. Around 680 of these were families with children.

→ Over the Christmas period more than 1,100 children will be homeless and living in temporary accommodation in Wales.

→ In 2014/15 more than 10 children became homeless in Wales every day.

FACT! Being homeless means not having somewhere

safe or suitable to live. This includes having to live in places that are unsafe, overcrowded or unaffordable. Between July and December 2015 there were 9,915 households presenting themselves as homeless to Welsh local authorities. This is many more than the number of people who were sleeping on the streets – estimated at 240 in November 2015.

FACT! Substance misuse is quite common among people sleeping rough: around two-thirds of rough sleepers cite drug or alcohol use as a reason for first becoming homeless. However, there are also many rough sleepers who don't have a drug or alcohol problem. For example, one study found that 27% of homeless people had or were recovering from an alcohol problem, while 39% said they took drugs or were recovering from a drug problem. Of those surveyed, half said that they used drugs and/or alcohol to cope with mental health issues.

FACT! A survey by the National Audit Office in 2007 found that just under 5% of veterans had experienced homelessness since leaving the armed forces. There is evidence that some people may find it hard to adjust to a life outside the military, through factors such as the trauma of combat, the mobility of the job or the drinking culture. Although people who have served in the armed forces have extra rights to housing as a priority need group, they only qualify for this extra help if they are homeless at the point of discharge. If they become homeless after having left the forces, they are eligible for the same level of help as everyone else.

FACT! Homelessness is not a lifestyle choice. Being homeless is brutally tough: homeless people are 13 times more likely to be a victim of violent crime than the general public, and 47 times more likely to be a victim of theft. A person sleeping rough is 35 times more likely to commit suicide than the average person. The vast majority of people sleeping rough are doing so not out of choice but out of necessity.

There is help available for people who are struggling to keep a roof over their head. But it's so important to seek help early – the earlier you do this, the more easily problems can be solved.

Here are nine signs that a friend or work colleague may be at risk of losing their home:

1. Have they recently had a relationship breakdown? This could separate the household and threaten the tenancy.
2. Do they seem to be struggling financially? Are they trying to save money on basics such as food or transport? This may mean they are also struggling to cover their rent or mortgage.
3. Have they spoken about the condition of their home? Perhaps they can't afford repairs. This could affect their health or even make the home too dangerous to live in.

4. Have terms and conditions changed in their workplace? Have they had their hours reduced or been made redundant? This could impact on their ability to pay bills.

5. Are they having health problems, physical or mental? This could affect their ability to deal with everyday matters, and their home could become unsuitable for their needs.

6. Have they spoken of the difficulty of finding a home? A person may be struggling to find a suitable property they can afford due to high fees, rents or set-up costs.

7. Are they changing jobs? This could affect their income. If their accommodation is tied to their job they may need to find somewhere else to live urgently.

8. Has there been a change in government policies that would affect them? Changes such as the benefit cap could leave them facing hardship even if they've been managing fine so far.

9. Has there been a change in their household? If there's a new addition to the family or if someone moves out, this could affect the household income.

Shelter Cymru believes everybody in Wales deserves a decent, secure home: it is the foundation for the health and well-being of people and communities. Shelter Cymru helps people in Wales every year struggling with bad housing or homelessness and we campaign to prevent it in the first place. We are there so that no one has to deal with bad housing or homelessness on their own.

Congratulations on completing a 2018 Quick Read.

The Quick Reads project, with bite-sized books, is designed to get readers back into the swing of reading, and reading for pleasure. So we sincerely hope you enjoyed this book.

Got an opinion?

Your feedback can make this project better. Now you've read one of the Quick Reads series visit www.readingwales.org.uk or Twitter @quickreads2018 to post your feedback.

→ Why did you choose this book?

→ What did you like about it?

→ What do you think of the Quick Reads series?

→ Which Quick Reads would you like to see in the future?

What next?

Now that you've finished one Quick Read – got time for another? Look out for the other title in the 2018 Quick Reads series – *Words Apart* by Llinos Dafydd

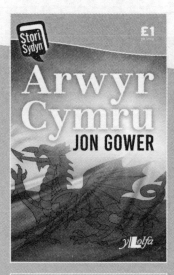

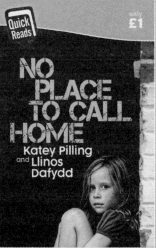
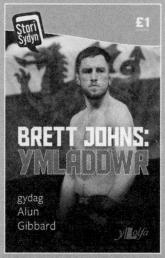

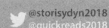